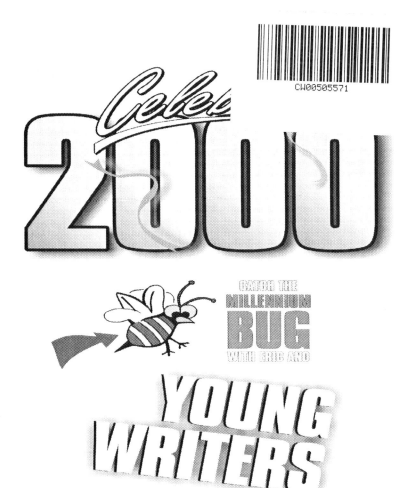

CW00505571

WIGAN

Edited by Michelle Warrington

First published in Great Britain in 1999 by
YOUNG WRITERS
Remus House,
Coltsfoot Drive,
Woodston,
Peterborough, PE2 9JX
Telephone (01733) 890066

HB ISBN 0 75431 526 6
SB ISBN 0 75431 527 4

FOREWORD

Young Writers have produced poetry books in conjunction with schools for over eight years; providing a platform for talented young people to shine. This year, the Celebration 2000 collection of regional anthologies were developed with the millennium in mind.

With the nation taking stock of how far we have come, and reflecting on what we want to achieve in the future, our anthologies give a vivid insight into the thoughts and experiences of the younger generation.

We were once again impressed with the quality and attention to detail of every entry received and hope you will enjoy the poems we have decided to feature in *Celebration 2000 Wigan* for many years to come.

CONTENTS

Hindley Green CP School

Gemma Crank	29
Christopher Doxey	30
Dean Podmore	31
Jonathan Carr	32
Chris Kenyon	33
Josh Mellors	34
Rachel Biggy	35
Claire Halsall	36
Sophia Wain	37
Ben Partington	38
Kim Findley	39
Craig Abbott	40
Scott Rothwell	41
Stacey Atherton	42
Bethany Wood	43
James Smith	44
Michael Farron	45
Terrin Turner	46

Marsh Green CP School

Laura Vasseur	47
Lauren Boardman	48
Daniel Gaskell	49
Katie Tracey	50
Tracey Halsall	51
Kurtis Shaw	52
Scott Unsworth	53
Lucy Waddicar	54
Emma Thompson	55
Thomas Frodsham	56
Christopher Dean	57
Aaron Hardman	58
Stacey Marcroft	59

St Lukes's CE Primary School, Lowton,

Emily Part	60
Stuart Burrows	61

The Poems

A HUMAN MACHINE

In the attic
In the new house
The speaking scanner
The stomping of the laptop computer
The giggles and laughs of the speakers
The screen bouncing up and down

The computer cards jumping on the keyboard
And the keyboard shaking off the cards
The spaghetti wires crawling all on the floor
And paper zooming out of the printer.

James Littler (8)
Beech Hill CP School

THE DESERT

I can hear something coming
It's quiet and soft
It is the desert wind
It's a small breeze rushing across my face
It's cool and it's refreshing
I wish I could have a nice drink
Of still cold water with some ice
Juicy fruit
I could drink a coconut
Under a palm tree, I could
Share it with the monkeys and
Lizards that crawl over the rocks
Oh no! What do I see? Some
Poachers chasing that monkey
I shall have to save it
I ran as fast as I could
I caught the monkey and climbed
Up a tree and hid there till
The poachers went.

Philip Orme (9)
Beech Hill CP School

LOOKING CLOSELY

Look up
Look down
Look side to side
What is it?
I don't know!
Kneel closely, take a look
Go closer and closer
Smell it, touch, it, taste it.
It's a beautiful day.

Melanie Hibbs (9)
Beech Hill CP School

WEATHER WEATHER

It's raining today, what a poor day
It's sunny today, what a rich day
It's winter today, what a terrible day
It's summer today, what a bright day
It's stormy today, what a black day
It's spring today, what a green day
It's breezy today, what a blue and fresh day
Weather, weather, what can you say?
You just can't get away from it
It's with you every day.

Emily Fearnley (9)
Beech Hill CP School

LEAVES

A little brown boat floating
On a pond
No, just a leaf
Sleeping on the
Shimmering water
Fluttering by

A multi-coloured leaf
Flying in the treetops
No, just a butterfly
Flashes of emerald and azure
Peeping through the shadowy
Sunshine.

Rebecca Eaton (9)
Beech Hill CP School

FUTURE

What will it be like 100 years from now?
Will there be food to eat and drinks to drink?
Will there still be animals to love?
Will there be fancy clothes or boring clothes?
And will there still be brick houses or
Will there be metal houses?
Will there still be pollution and cars
Chugging up the roads and will there
Still be education for children?

Danielle Lenahan (8)
Birchley St Mary's RC Primary School

FUTURE

What will it be like 100 years from now?
Will there be good zappers to zap food when you're hungry?
Will you be able to travel by submarine
To underwater school and holidays?
Will houses be made of sweets and no gravity
And will people live in space?
Will there be football, rugby and all other sports?
Will there be home tutors if there is no school?
Will scientists invent teleporters and time machines?
Will people fly to space with rocket booster packs?
Will there be solar-powered houses and robotic pencils?
Will there be everlasting gum and flavoured food pills?
Will there be any of these things?
Will anybody find out?

James Smith (8)
Birchley St Mary's RC Primary School

MY FUTURE 2000!

In a hundred years what will there be?
A giant teleporter waiting for me.

Will you be able to live in space?
Will man discover a brand new place?

Will there be everlasting gums?
Will there be robotic mums?

Will you be able to travel in a submarine?
Will the grass still be green?

Will there be a Space Hotel?
Will a computer look after me when I'm not well?

Will countries go cold near the equator?
Will there be a remote controled waiter?

Nicholas Murphy (9)
Birchley St Mary's RC Primary Schoo

MY PREDICTIONS

I'm predicting the future
Many years from now,
I'll ask lots of questions like
Why? What? and How?

I can see every movement about to be made,
I can see every board game about to be played.

I can look into a crystal ball
And tell you when you're going to fall.

There's a few more questions I have to know
Because it's nearly time for me to go.

Will there be gravity in 100 years?
Will the world be full of tears?

I like predicting, I really do
And if you did my job, I'm sure you would, too.

I'm saying goodbye now, but don't be sad
Because I know you can take it, it's not that bad.

Rebecca Cunliffe (9)
Birchley St Mary's RC Primary School

MY DOG

My dog is as fast as the speed of light
His body glistens during the night,
He's bright, he's cheery as can be
As you can guess, he's very special to me.

His fur is silky and pretty
But it is such a pity,
He's a mongrel dog and afraid of the fog
And very scratchy.

Lorna Forrester (7)
Birchley St Mary's RC Primary School

MY PET CAT

I have a pet cat,
She sits on a mat,
One day she chased my mouse
Around the house.
I got so mad,
I told my dad,
And he threw her away

And that day,
I was very sad,
So I told my dad.

He told me to go outside and look for her,
So I went outside and looked for her.
I found my cat,
Sitting on the outside mat.

Emily Collins (8)
Birchley St Mary's RC Primary School

RED DWARF

On Red Dwarf you'll meet the Cat
He's cool, silly but quite fat.
There's Holly The Hologram and two silly men
One's so dumb he can't use a pen.

Red Dwarf is red, I expect you know
And that's why their favourite Telly Tubby is Po.
One man has an H on his head
His teapot, his plate and even his bed.

Carrie Sinnott Clark (8)
Birchley St Mary's RC Primary School

MY CAT

I've got a cat called Kitty,
She messes with my Aunt Nitty,
She plays with her day and night,
Sometimes she gives a very hard bite.
She plays in my bed,
She won't be fed.

I said, "Oh, Kitty, what have you done?"
She plays with the water gun.
Me and Kitty have apple pie,
So now it's time to say *goodbye.*

Rebecca Swift (7)
Birchley St Mary's RC Primary School

GOOD DAYS

Waking up in a big duvet
With a cosy bed,
The sun shining brightly
Just over my head.

Seeing all the puddles disappear
I know this is a good day 'cause
Summer is near.

In the afternoon
I had a chocolate ice-cream
When it melted
It was a wave machine.

With my pocket money
I bought a yellow balloon
It looked like
Another sun.

Later on the sun drove past
Bringing the moon
With a glistening blast.

The moon came rolling along
As if a famous footballer
Had kicked it into the air
Where it stuck there
And in the morn
It waved bye bye.

Louise Calleja (10)
Birchley St Mary's RC Primary School

A BAD DAY

A bad day is
>   a cut knee,
A bad day is
>   a toothache,
A bad day is
>   going to the dentist,
A bad day is
>   a deflated balloon,
A bad day is
>   dried-up snow,
A bad day is
>   a wet day,
A bad day is
>   a headache,
A bad day is
>   an earache,
A bad day is
>   a cold winter's night,
A bad day is
>   a night,
A bad day is
>   a pen with no ink.

Layla Horton (9)
Birchley St Mary's RC Primary School

SATURDAY GOOD DAY

Saturday is warm.
Saturday is homework in a fire.
Saturday is TV world.
Saturday is Playstation day.
Saturday is fizzy water day.
Saturday is no hard work day.
Saturday is mint ice-cream with chocolate chips.

Sinead Chisholm (9)
Birchley St Mary's RC Primary School

BLUE

Blue is like a blueberry
      Cut and ready to eat
Blue is the colour of the sea
      With the waves swishing up and down.
Blue is the colour of the cloudy sky
      Moving round and round.
Blue is the taste of bubblegum
      Popping in your mouth.
Blue smells like chlorine
      Out of the swimming pool.
Blue is the colour of my school uniform
      When it has been washed and ironed.
Blue is the colour of Matthew housepoints
      to be won.
Blue is the colour of my hair bobble
      Glistening in the sun.
Blue is the colour of my eyes
      Shining in the shade.
Blue is the colour of my tray
      With my name tag on.
Blue is the colour of my best pen
      of Bugs Bunny.

Rebecca Coleman (9)
Birchley St Mary's RC Primary School

RED

Red is an apple
      Juicy as can be.
Red is the sunset
      At 6.00pm.
Red is a hot rock
      In a volcano.
Red is a siren
      Alerting all the soldiers.
Red is a fire
      Burning all the crops.
Red is the blood
      From a dead animal.
Red is a cloak
      Taming the bulls.

Christopher Moore (10)
Birchley St Mary's RC Primary School

FRIENDS

Without friends what would we do?
The world would be a nasty place for me and you.

Everybody needs friends to share,
Friends will care.

Friends make the world a better place,
It's nice to see a friend's smiling face.

Martin Sharrock (7)
Garswood CP School

LIMERICK

There once was a pig called Bert
Who rolled around in the dirt,
He got a big blister,
And sat on his sister,
Then it really started to hurt!

Gary Owen (11)
Garswood CP School

LIMERICK

There once was a man called Ned,
Who liked to chew on his bed,
He snapped the bed's rail,
And went rather pale,
When he found it was made out of lead!

Alix Warbuton (10)
Garswood CP School

I LOVE FOOD

I n the cupboards,

L ovely tins of potatoes,
O ozing tomato sauce,
V ariety of unusual breakfast cereals,
E very colour of jelly cube.

F antastic fruits from around the world,
O bserve the soggy honey,
O xo cubes waiting to be made into gravy,
D elicious home-made biscuits.

Scott Dean (10)
Garswood CP School

I LOVE FOOD

I n the icy freezer there's my favourite food,

L ike chocolate, ice pops and lovely things,
O ranges lemons and apples in the fruit bowl,
V icious vegetables being chopped on the table,
E verlasting Dime Bars get stuck in your teeth.

F ruit juice oozing out of the can,
O rangey carrots out of the vegetable family,
O val plates filled right up with food,
D elicious crisps bursting out of the bag.
> *Gulp it down now!*

Rosemary Ansell (10)
Garswood CP School

MY FAVOURITE THINGS

The yellow of the blazing hot sun.
Frosty, cold, damp winter.
Amazing, sunny, smooth Spain.
Roasting hot summer's morning.
A pair of silky baggy trousers.
Comfy night-time, cosy bed.
The galloping exciting horse-riding show.
Crunchy, crumbly chocolate biscuits.

Hannah Blackburn
Garswood CP School

THE MAN FROM BOMBAY

There was a man from Bombay,
Who ate a big barrel of hay,
He fell down on his back,
With a bone-breaking crack,
And that was his very last day!

Thomas Middleton (11)
Garswood CP School

SEASON OF DECAY

Autumn is here,
The season of decay,
Pale ghostly fungi,
Peeping cautiously,
Through the soft earth,
Golden leaves,
Glide down gracefully,
Yellow, russet and orange,
Bare trees stand silently,
Like bare skeleton bones,
All bare,
Winter will soon be here!

Zoe Jones (16)
Garswood CP School

FLICKERING FLAMES

Flickering flames dancing in the moonlight,
The hot wax dripping down slowly,
Lighting up the whole room,
Everlasting till the night is out,
Burning down slowly,
Until the candle is extinguished!

Laura Collins (11)
Garswood CP School

MACHINES

Washing machines whirling
Like a fierce tornado,
Lawn mowers chewing
The long juicy grass,
Radio thumping
A Spice Girls beat
Like a big metal drum
Buzzing in my ears,
Vacuum cleaners churning
Like bikes revving furiously,
Computer printers beeping
As the pages pour out,
Inter City speed trains
Stopping at the platforms,
Aeroplanes whooshing through the air,
At a mighty speed with a line of vapour,
Traffic lights flashing on and off
Like the stars twinkling in the sky,
Microwaves ting as mums cook food,
Cars and lorries zooming
Along the motorway,
Like an aeroplane taking off into the sky,
Telephones ringing
Like a fire alarm,
Radios 'shouting', 'laughing'
'Whisper' or 'talk'
Farmer in the tractor
Ploughing the field
Like a food mixer
Whisking round the food,
Machines are all around us,
They're everywhere we look!

Amanda Lee (11)
Garswood CP School

MICE

Beware . . .
Mice will attack
They are usually small
and
cute
with
a
long
thin
pink
tail.

But my mouse is a monster.
It chews at my fingers
It chews at my toes
It even chews at my homework
That Miss gave me to do.

It gets bigger and bigger each day
I just hope it doesn't eat me for dinner.

Gemma Crank (10)
Hindley Green CP School

WEATHER

Lightning cracked in the distance
Thunder banged like a drum
The snow is as cold as water
The sun is a big ball of fire
The rain making big puddles
Mean black clouds getting ready to kill.

Christopher Doxey (9)
Hindley Green CP School

SEASONS

January's full of rain and snow
February's full of winds that blow.
March is just the same, I guess
April is quite different though.
May brings the pleasant sun
June is full of the blazing sun
July says, 'I'm here to stay'
August brings beautiful breezes
September fruits are gathered in.
October comes and brings the gales
November bonfires burn way
December comes and it's
Christmas.

Dean Podmore (10)
Hindley Green CP School

ANIMALS IN THE WILD

A big, goldy, yellow lion
Is roaring in soaking wet rain.

Two big brown bears
Are fighting near a waterfall.

On the white, smooth sand
A green, slithering snake is wriggling along.

The giraffe's neck is as long as a tree.

A small black monkey
Is washing himself in the small, cool pool.

A baby tiger is walking with his
Black and orange-striped mum.

Jonathan Carr (10)
Hindley Green CP School

ROLLERBLADES

Rollerblades are fast
Cool
And fun.
They've got laces, straps and
Wheels.
It's a great sport,
With flat-out fun,
You can do stunts like
Royal grind, bio air 360
And front side soul revert.
Blades are like a train on a
Railway track.
Wheels come in all kinds of sizes
And colours.

Chris Kenyon (9)
Hindley Green CP School

WEATHER

Weather so cold and wet
It makes me shiver.
When it rains at school I really hate it
Because we cannot play out.
When it snows at the weekend
I like it because I can play out.
When it is hot I like it because
I can play out.
When it is icy I like it because
I can have fun on the ice.
Whatever the weather is like, I like it.

Josh Mellors (10)
Hindley Green CP School

FAMILY

My family is just great
They cuddle you like a teddy bear
They give you money to spend
My family is always there for me
My family is the best thing in the world
I love my family more than anything.

Rachel Biggy (10)
Hindley Green CP School

MY MUM

My mum helps me
She is kind to me
She talks to me
When I am upset.

She always buys me
What I ask her for
She sings like a summer bird
In the sky.

Claire Halsall (10)
Hindley Green CP School

WEATHER

On Monday the sun shone like a bright torch in the sky
On Tuesday the rain slavered like a baby down the window
On Wednesday the thunder banged on the door like a businessman
On Thursday the snow fell like icing sugar on a cake
On Friday the ice froze the pond like a silver disc
On Saturday it thawed like a defrosting loaf
On Sunday the weather was just fine.

Sophia Wain (9)
Hindley Green CP School

SPACE

Space is where other planets lie
Like Saturn with its rings
Like Frisbees floating around
And Jupiter with its red dot.

Spaceships are flying everywhere
Look at the sun
Phew that's hot!
Look at Venus the cloudy planet.

Ben Partington (10)
Hindley Green CP School

GROMIT

Gromit is my hamster
And he smells of sawdust.
He is the size of a small carrot.
Gromit's fur is the colour of my hair.
When he bites it feels like a pair of
Pliers digging into me,
Owwwwwww Gromit!

Kim Findley (9)
Hindley Green CP School

AMERICAN FOOTBALL

Emmit celebrates after he's scored,
He jumps up and looks at the board.
The score is 20-20
The team wants to get past 40.
They kicked the ball
And shouted, 'Goal!'
At the end of the match
Emmit said, 'We won!'

Craig Abbott (9)
Hindley Green CP School

DADS

Dads always help you,
Dads like to fix cars.
They like playing on computers.
My dad is always there for me.
Dads like watching Formula 1
And touring cars on TV.

Scott Rothwell (10)
Hindley Green CP School

THE SEAGULL

Penguins are black, white and yellow
They make me jealous on purpose
Eating the fish from the sea
Which are mine.

Then I fly away till suddenly
I stop again
And I see some seals being lazy.
They should be more like me
Looking for food for their children.

Then I fly away again
And stop
As I see my prey
Down I fly and then
Snap!
I've got them
And off I fly again.

Stacey Atherton (9)
Hindley Green CP School

RAINFOREST

The sun goes behind the clouds
All goes quiet, the birds stop singing.
Animals run for shelter as the storm is coming.

The thunder shakes the ground.
The rain pours down as if from a jug
Flashes of lightning and rumbles of thunder.

Then all goes quiet
The storm has passed
And birds begin to sing.

Bethany Wood (10)
Hindley Green CP School

RALLY CARS

Roaring down the track
Like a lion running through the jungle.
They spin and they hit the crash barrier.
Their tyres are smoking when they drive
Into the pitstop.

Rally cars zooming round the track
As fast as a rocket on wheels.

James Smith (9)
Hindley Green CP School

YEAR 2000 CELEBRATIONS

If there is a party, include me.
I love parties
The food
The drink
Games like pass the parcel
And statues.
When there's music
I have to dance
I like singing to songs
Remember
When there is a party
Include me.

Michael Farron (10)
Hindley Green CP School

SORROW

When I have a broken heart I feel sorrow
When I see orphans I feel sorrow
If the sun goes down I feel sorrow.

May it always be Valentine's Day
May it always be June the 10th
May it always be my day.

Terrin Turner (9)
Hindley Green CP School

BRIGHT-COLOURED RAINBOWS

Rainbows, rainbows,
Bright-coloured rainbows,
Reds, oranges, yellows and blues,
High in the sky the rainbow goes.

Rainbows, rainbows,
Bright-coloured rainbows,
Feint to see, cute as can be,
Then the rain starts to pour.

Rainbows, rainbows,
Bright-coloured rainbows,
The sun comes out and dries the rain
So the rainbow goes home again.

Rainbows, rainbows,
Bright-coloured rainbows,
Reds, oranges, yellows and blues,
High in the sky the rainbow goes.

Laura Vasseur (10)
Marsh Green CP School

DREAMING DOG

This little dog all alone
Sits in his kennel and dreams of a bone.
Chewing and crunching
Imagine that he
Thinks to himself
He's a cat
His name is Felix,
He's black and white,
He doesn't want to
Look like a cat.

Now he's dreaming he is
A bird high in the sky
Following the herd
Chattering in his sleep,
Blue tit, robin and goldfinch
Lapping water from the bird bath.

Imagine that he is
Nibbling that crunchy bread,
Eating worms.
Yuk! No thank you.

I'll be a dog
The same as I am,
Sitting in my kennel, dreaming all day.

Lauren Boardman (9)
Marsh Green CP School

THE DRIPPING WATER

Dripping water making sounds,
Clitty, clatty, wibble, wobble.
Dripping water out of the tap
Drip, drop, down the sink.
Flooding water in the house,
Making the house flood everywhere.
Put the water in the bath,
Splish, splash and have a good soak.
Put some water in your cup
And have a good drink.

Daniel Gaskell (9)
Marsh Green CP School

ONOMATOPOEIA POETRY

Creak, crack, bang,
I get into the spaceship
And off we go.

The spaceship
Starts to zap
And shake
And we land onto Pluto.

Bubbling, boiling,
Sizzling, fizzling,
Scorching, splutter
Splat
I want to get
Out of here!

Eek, ah, wallop,
I land straight onto an alien.
He doesn't like me
And turns me into
A human lolly.
Then I pop into my
Right size and I go
Straight home!

Katie Tracey (9)
Marsh Green CP School

WHAT IS . . . . . FRIENDSHIP?

Friendship is two boats
      joined for eternal life

Friendship is a person
      who sticks beside you forever

Friendship is a kind of peace
      burning in and out of us

Friendship is a potion
      no one can ever see

Friendship is a cord
      that's pulled when it is needed

Friendship is always inside us
      but someone special brings it out.

Tracey Halsall (10)
Marsh Green CP School

FRIENDSHIP IS . . . .

Friendship is a car going on and on
And when the fuel burns out
Your friendship is broken

It is a fire burning on and on
When you stop putting wood on
Your friendship has gone

It is a cable phone ringing on and on
If you don't pay the bill
They will cut you off

It is a computer
If you don't plug it in
It will never start.

Kurtis Shaw (10)
Marsh Green CP School

WINTER

Snowflakes falling to the ground,
Dancing, fluttering, to the ground.
Places freezing up,
Birds flying away.

People making snowmen,
Trees covered in flakes,
People making snowballs,
Then the snow melts away.

Scott Unsworth
Marsh Green CP School

CHEWY FRUIT GUMS

Orange, yellow, green, red and black,
Small and round and lumpy on top.
With a fruity smell,
Smooth all round.

Tastes like lime, orange, blackcurrant, strawberry and lemon,
When I eat them they make no noise
But just stick to my teeth
And won't come off.

Lucy Waddicar (11)
Marsh Green CP School

GALAXY

The hard brown squares
Smell sweet and chocolatey,
The smooth silky taste
They melt in my mouth.
When I chew them
They make no noise.
Galaxy chocolate,
I love it!

Emma Thompson (11)
Marsh Green CP School

TONGUE POPPERS

They're round and sweet
And rot your teeth.
They tickle your tongue
All day long.
They're very small to put in your pocket
They could even fit into a locket
Put them on your tongue and feel so sour
Because they have so much power.

Thomas Frodsham (11)
Marsh Green CP School

THE CARAMEL

The caramel is a teeth-destroyer
But the rich gold soft caramel
Drips from my mouth.
It melts in my wide mouth
Like butter in the sun,
It runs like shining honey
And is enjoyable to eat.

Christopher Dean (11)
Marsh Green CP School

MY EXPLANATION OF THE RAIN CYCLE

The sun warms up the water,
The water ascends and takes off.
The water's vapour constructs clouds.
The wind breezes the clouds.
The clouds feel the mountains.
The clouds cool and rain slashes down.
The clouds freeze and rain splashes down.
The rain streams off to the sea.

Aaron Hardman (10)
Marsh Green CP School

FRIENDSHIP

Friendship is a poem
That goes on and on.

Friendship is a shadow
That is by you everywhere.

It is always by your side
Everywhere you go, wherever you are.

Friendship is a watch,
Ticking away every day.

It is like a bracelet
Tying in a knot on your wrist.

It is a boat
That never stops wherever you're going.

Stacey Marcroft (11)
Marsh Green CP School

MY DOG JAKE

How can I describe my dog?
Oh yes, he has an oval for his body,
A circle for his head
And four little legs.

He walks slowly like a little old man
But when we give him his Pedigree Chum
He runs like an Olympic runner
To the finishing line.

When he was a puppy
He would jump in the washing machine
Now we have to pay
To get him washed!

He barks when the cat is in the garden
Or when someone walks past.
He looks cute, cuddly and furry
He has a twinkle in his eye when I look at him.

I like him because he's playful,
I like him because he's always my friend,
I like him because he's ginger blond,
Just like me.

Emily Part (9)
St Lukes's CE Primary School, Lowton

DOLPHINS

They're easy to draw, a half moon with fins, a tail and a snout
They're bluey-grey, sometimes with spots.
They glide stealthily through the water
Flipping up and down.
They jump and pull somersaults in the air
They're acrobats of the animal kingdom.
They work together to round up herring
Then they open their mouths as wide as they can
And gulp them down.
When they're happy, sad or scared
They click, echo or squeak.
They look smooth, smile a lot and are cute.
They have cone-shaped teeth.
I think they're cute, funny, intelligent and mysterious.
They are my favourite animals from the sea.

Stuart Burrows (9)
St Lukes's CE Primary School, Lowton

ICE-CREAM

I smile and I feel happy.
My tummy rumbles very loud.
I lick the ice-cream.
It is cold, sloppy and very sweet.
It slides down my throat.
It is so delicious.
I bite into the cone.
It is crispy, crunchy like a biscuit.
The cone is just like a microphone.
When I bite into the cone
My front teeth, they ache for a second.
I eat the last bit but I want another
Because it is so sweet.

Amie Parr (8)
St Lukes's CE Primary School, Lowton

THE FANTASTIC DREAM

I stare at the ice-cream.
I hover my nose over it.
The cold, sweet smell comes to my nose.
I lick it slowly.
It is sweet and sticky.
It trickles down my throat.
My tummy is screaming for it.
It slowly comes into my tummy.
My tummy is so happy it is laughing.
The sweet, sticky ice-cream comes rushing
At a hundred miles an hour.
Oh No! The ice-cream has run out
But what about the cone?
The cone is crispy, crunchy, golden, munchy.
The last bit . . . *crunch! Mmmm!.*

Michael Geeleher (9)
St Lukes's CE Primary School, Lowton

THE ICE-CREAM EXPERIENCE

I see the ice-cream.
My eyes stare down.
My taste buds prepare.
I slowly stick my tongue out.
Lick!
A scrumptious vanillary taste breaks into my mouth.
The ice-cream slips and slides down my throat
Like a child on a helter-skelter.
It reaches my stomach
I smile with glee.
I bite into the cone,
Crispy, crunchy, golden, munchy.
It tastes gorgeous.
Suddenly it disappears.
Oh no! I want another!

Gemma Cayton (9)
St Lukes's CE Primary School, Lowton

DINNER TIME

Say the Grace, fix my lace,
Say, 'Good morning, everyone.'
I shoot out like a bomb.
I see the dinners lining up,
I run around and I am puffed!
The whistle blows - 'Sandwiches, line up!'
I run to the line with my friends.
We walk round the corner. Oh no!
The door is locked. The dinner lady knocks.
Luckily there's someone inside.
'Two at a time, please.' It's Laura and me.
We go into the bathroom and out again.
We grab our lunchboxes and my mouth waters.
At my table, I eat my food,
Then run outside and pretend
I am a horse in a stable.
Ouch! I've cut my knee.
The boy who pushed me
Is on the wall.
The whistle blows, 'Line up.'
That's the fun over.

Rebecca Boardman (8)
St Lukes's CE Primary School, Lowton

DINNER TIME

We say the Grace
And, 'Good morning, everyone.'
(It's good to be stopping work)
I try to get out first.
I line up after dinner.
I am a sandwich person.
Will I be with my friend?
Where will I sit today?
We rush to the line.
I'm first. *Yes!*
My friend is with me.
I scoff my dinner down.
My friend is out before me.
Let's play cops and robbers.
We bump heads.
Just then the whistle goes.
Back to work!

Clare Douglas (8)
St Lukes's CE Primary School, Lowton

DINNER TIME

I rush outside,
Push and shove.
Here's room for Jodie,
Rebecca comes in the line,
Save a place for Danielle,
Here she is, just in time.
Jump up to the basketball hoop.
It's way too tall.
We sit with our dinners
And talk and talk and talk and talk.

Darcas Lever (8)
St Lukes's CE Primary School, Lowton

DINNER TIME

I wonder what's for dinner?
Mmm, chicken drummers!
When I get my food
I'm going to gobble it all up . . .
Guess what?
I'm up next!
My mouth waters,
My eyes gleam
At the mouth-watering food.
I take my knife and fork,
I stab into the chicken.
Mmmmmmmmmmmm!
May I have another one?
Sadly my dinner was all gone.

Danial Jones (8)
St Lukes's CE Primary School, Lowton

DINNER TIME

I'm in the classroom, saying the Grace,
I'm in the classroom, tying my lace,
For swimming, I take off my tie,
(Be careful - keep my points count high).
I'm now waiting for my dinner,
Hurray, I'm first, I'm a winner!
Hear those chicken drummers drumming,
Drumming as loud as can be?
Brilliant, I'm next to my friends,
This is the place, just right for me!

Anthony Unzueta (8)
St Lukes's CE Primary School, Lowton

DINNER TIME

Say the Grace,
'Morning, everyone,'
Rush out of the room,
Run into the bathroom,
Show my hands to the tap,
Zoom to the line,
Hope I'm with my friends,
In the dinner hall at last.
Nearly my turn,
Is it my favourite?
What should I have for dessert?
'Strawberry yoghurt, please.'
Eating my dinner,
Want to get out.
Good, I've finished now.
Walk to the hatch,
Put my tray down,
Skip outside, play a game.
Oh, now the whistle's gone!
Line up and go inside.

Jodie Heaton (8)
St Lukes's CE Primary School, Lowton

DINNER TIME

I say the Grace,
Good morning, everyone,
Get out earliest,
Show hands to the tap.
Pleasing food - fish cake -
Mmmmm!
Will I be next to a friend?
Where will I sit?
Jokes with the kitchen staff,
It's a jolly life for me!
Dinner is finished,
It's out to play
Cops and robbers or tig,
Which one today?
Oh no, the whistle has gone
But I've not fallen over!
Hurray!

Danielle Duddle (8)
St Lukes's CE Primary School, Lowton

DINNER TIME

I say the Grace,
We say, 'Good morning,'
We show the tap our hands.
I rush into the line.
I'm first!
But where is my friend?
He is behind me.
The teacher is letting us in.
The cook is saying a joke!
I get a table, my friend follows me.
I go out to play.
I play football or cops and robbers.
I hate getting hurt
Or put on the wall.
But I like dinner time.

Christopher Jenkins (7)
St Lukes's CE Primary School, Lowton

DINNER TIME

I say the Grace,
I run out of my place.
I make my way
To go out to play.
I am in a good mood
For lovely food.
I rush back inside
And show my hands to the tap.
I run to get my lunch box
And eat like a hungry fox.
I go out to play a game -
The whistle - oh no - back inside again!

Laura Edwards (7)
St Lukes's CE Primary School, Lowton

SCHOOL DINNERS

We hate

S limy spaghetti,
C heap corned beef,
H orrible ham,
O ozing onions,
O ily olives,
L umpy lettuce.

D etestable doughnuts,
I nedible ice cream,
N asty noodles,
N auseous nuggets,
E vil eggs,
R evolting rice pudding,
S chool Dinners.

Hannah Doherty (11)
Shevington CP School

MILLENNIUM

The millennium is nearly here,
It's less than a year.

The parties will be in full swing
With everyone doing their own thing.

The drinks will flow
And fireworks will glow.

People will shout and scream
Children will eat ice-cream.

The millennium is nearly here,
It's less than a year.

Sean Waring (11)
Shevington CP School

RAINY DAYS

The blue sky turns grey,
It's a start of a rainy day.
Raindrops patter down my window,
Racing each other down the pane.
Time to put on my coat and wellies
And don't forget my umbrella.
I can splash in puddles, Mum won't mind
Because the sun is peeping through
And there is a rainbow too.

Clare Louise Mitchell (11)
Shevington CP School

My Trainer

I've made good friends with my trainer.
We talk all day and night,
He's a shiny Ellesse trainer
With sides green and white.

We talk about mountains and faraway lands
And he can do quite a lot
For a guy with no hands.

But long white laces wound up in each hole
Which he used in a football match
To score the winning goal.

Caroline Waterworth (11)
Shevington CP School

CATS

P u r r r r r r f e c t i o n!
Some cats are small and
Some cats are big
Beautiful glowing eyes,
Soft, furry, cute and cuddly.
All cats are intelligent and have 9 lives.
I love cats.
They sit in front of the fire with a coiled tail.
They are hunters, they *c r e e p* upon their prey.
Cats are lovable creatures, round, thin, fast and exotic.
Tabbies, Siamese and Persians are the breeds I like most
But I love all cats.

Sarah Vidler (11)
Shevington CP School

THE SEASONS

In the spring all the trees start to bud,
All the animals begin to feel good.
All the birds come back to sing,
This is how we know it's spring.

In the summer the flowers begin to bloom,
People are no longer filled with gloom.
Smiling faces all around,
No longer pointing at the ground.

The autumn leaves turn to gold,
They crinkle as they grow old.
As they tumble off the trees,
You will find many colours of leaves.

The winter time has come again
And it has brought the heavy rain.
It's also started to go cold
But in the sky the sun shines gold.

There's something nice about each season,
For every one there's a different reason.
Each day I pray to God above
And thank Him for the world we love.

Thomas Sudworth (10)
Shevington CP School

SUMMER

Summer is a time when the air is hot,
Unless you live in England and then it's not.

Monday to Sunday lying on beaches,
Midsummer trees holding juicy peaches.

Early in the morning birds sing
Rather hear that than hear the bell ring.

James Fisher (11)
Shevington CP School

HORSES

Horses running on the plains,
With flying tails and tossing manes.
Then wake up again to feed and run
And bask beneath the midday sun.

Hear thunder of the herds,
The winging wonder of the birds.
See flowers with petals dewy bright,
Then darkness
And then the star-crazed night.

Laura Holt (11)
Shevington CP School

MY DOG, BLUE

My dog Blue, he's full of mischief.
He'd bite your shoe, he looks so blue.
He likes to bark, when the room is silent.

My dog Blue is a Great Dane pup,
He's 12 weeks old and he's as mad as can be.
His bone is big and hard,
He likes to chew it hard and loud.

Blue would chew it night and day
He likes to annoy you, that's my Blue.

Natalie Margaret Whittle (11)
Shevington CP School

IN MY HEAD

In my head . . .

. . . there is a fast-flowing river full of rubbish
Such as computers and junk food.
There is a clock counting down to the end of my life
And an unread E-Mail or an unchewed bar of chocolate.

. . . there is a sea of thoughts that slows anywhere,
Mixing all the thoughts up.
There is a memory span of about five whole seconds
For very important things.

. . . there is a big black space where a brain should be
But instead there is a secret box that is never locked.
There are very few emotions in the box
Other than pain, anguish and sarcasm.

. . . there are many, many thoughts and none of them
Are anything to do with this poem.
The many thoughts are all to do with
Happiness, enjoyment and entertainment.

Shaun Murdock (11)
Shevington CP School

FIFA '98

When I'm on FIFA '98 I'm *Brazil*,
I enter a friendly match.
The venue is Wembley,
The two clashing teams are
Brazil and *Argentina*.
It's lovely weather for football,
Nice and sunny.
The match kicks off with a fiery start,
Ronaldo sees that the goalie is off his line
And tries to lob the keeper
But it rattles the crossbar.
25 minutes into the game,
Denilson makes a break
But is forced to put a through ball to *Ronaldo*.
He nutmegs one defender and takes it round another,
He drills it into the top corner,
The keeper had no chance at all,
What a goal!
50 minutes into the game *Batistuta* scores with a header.
10 minutes from time,
Rivaldo scores a fabulous overhead,
The fans go wild!!!!
The full time whistle goes and the score ends up 2-1,
The fans go home happy after this match.

Greg Winnard (11)
Shevington CP School

WITCHES

Through the trees in the night
Sheltered by the pale moonlight
Stood the witch in her pointy hat
Mumbling spells to her magic black cat.

Her long, ugly nose
Gave me cold toes.
Her sharp fingernails
Made my face go very pale.

She caught me with her beady eye
And shouted out, 'you little spy.'
She gave me an evil glare
And then began to stare and stare.

When she began to grin at me
I knew she'd have me for her tea.
As the cauldron began to bubble
I realised I was in terrible trouble.

Tiffany Daniels (11)
Shevington CP School

TOCA

When I race a touring car this is what I see . . .
A Peugeot in the barrier,
A Renault ahead of me,
A Vectra going for victory
But I just watch and see.
A Honda ahead of the Vectra
But the Vectra gets him back.
Off goes the Honda right into the gravel trap.
Who is going to win this close race?
I just keep it at a steady pace.

Joseph Hodgson (10)
Shevington CP School

POP FEVER

Planet Pop's got a cool groove
Like cool live and kicking
And all the coolest pop stars
Nearly the biggest entertainments ever,
Even all the boring people think it's good.
Totally the best songs like 'Goodbye'

Pop, pop, pop is the coolest thing.
Our biggest hits in the galaxy
Plant Pop's the coolest ever.

Lucy Charlotte Cattle (10)
Shevington CP School

FROM SUNRISE TO SUNSET

Out of my window I can see
A crystal sky like the deep blue ocean,
Laughing children with not a care in the world,
Green, green grass like soft green velvet.

From sunrise to sunset I can see
The twisted trees like an old gnarled hand,
The huge bright sun like a sparkling gem,
A mysterious building where nobody goes.

Who is out there?
Nobody knows.

Ryan Barker (11)
Shevington CP School

NIGHT-TIME NOISES

I'm half-asleep, lying in bed,
Noises outside confusing my head.
Is it a ghost that gave me a fright?
Or is it an owl hooting in the night?
I hear a scream from outside,
I pull my covers over my head to hide.
Then I realise it is only a car
In the distance, driving afar.
Shadows of a swaying tree,
Is it a witch trying to frighten me?
Slowly I drift off to sleep,
Keep opening my eyes to have a peep.
Is there a monster under my bed?
Or is it a goblin with a green head?

Jessica Xavier (11)
Shevington CP School

MY RABBIT

I have a rabbit white as snow
His eyes are red and really glow
At night he comes inside to play
But stays outside during the day.
He has a hutch where he sleeps
And through the wire he likes to peep
Wondering if he's going to be fed
Or have his nose tickled instead.
He runs in the garden in the sun
Free as a bird, not in a run
A magpie came and pecked at him
As he was lying, oh so prim,
He just got up and turned around
And looked at him without a sound.
The bird got the message and flew away
And Snowy enjoyed the rest of the day.

Leanne Danson (10)
Shevington CP School

THE MILLENNIUM

The millennium is a thousand years,
In that time there's been lots of tears.

All the computers are shutting down,
The Millennium Bug has come to town.

Pills and potions, creams and lotions
Will not cure this plague.

Scientists, teachers and all kinds of preachers
Insist on being vague.

Tom Lowe (10)
Shevington CP School

WHAT SHALL I DO?

What shall I do? Write a poem.
What shall I do? Go back home.
What shall I do? Give a smile.
What shall I do? Wait a while.
What shall I do? Chase a mouse.
What shall I do? Buy a house.
What shall I do? Climb a tree.
What shall I do? Shout with glee.
What shall I do? Wear a hat.
What shall I do? Weave a mat.
What shall I do? Buy and sell.
What shall I do? Use hair gel.
What shall I do? Make some loaves.
What shall I do? Wear some clothes.
What shall I do? Use the bin.
What shall I do? Make a din.
What shall I do? Snip and snap.
What shall I do? Take a nap!

Stephanie Elizabeth Coupe (10)
Shevington CP School